BL: 5.4
AR Pts: 0.5
Test# 70797

The Atlas of the Seven Continents™

AFRICA

Wendy Vierow

The Rosen Publishing Group's

PowerKids Press™

New York

For Chris, who loves atlases

Published in 2004 by The Rosen Publishing Group, Inc.
29 East 21st Street, New York, NY 10010

First Edition

Editor: Frances E. Ruffin
Book Design: Maria E. Melendez

Photo Credits: Cover and title page, map of Africa, p. 5 © Earth Observatory/NASA; p. 5 (bottom maps) illustrated by Maria Melendez; p. 7 © 2001 Todd Marshall; p. 9 (map symbols), p. 15 (map of Africa) illustrated by Eric DePalo; pp. 9, 11, 13, 17 (map of Africa), 19 (right maps), 21 (left maps) © GeoAtlas; pp. 11 (Egypt, Nile Delta, and Sinai), (The Congo Basin, Africa's Great Lakes) © Jacques Descloitres; p. 11 (Mt. Kilimanjaro's Receding Glaciers) © Shuttle photograph provided by the Earth Sciences and Image Analysis Laboratory, Johnson Space Center; p. 17 (Addax Close-up) © Steve Kaufman/CORBIS; p. 17 (Fruit of Cacao Tree, Trinidad) © Franz-Marc Frei/CORBIS; p. 17 (Banana Tree) © Kennan Ward/CORBIS; p. 17 (lion, gorilla, zebra, cheetah, elephant, gorilla and giraffe) © Artville; p. 19 (Libyan oil field) © National Geographic Image Collection; p. 19 (Fishing in Sierra Leone) © Charles & Josette Lenars/CORBIS; p. 19 (Cocoa Harvest), p. 21 (Gambia, Algeria) © SuperStock; p. 21 (Masai girl) © Getty Images/Stone.

Vierow, Wendy.
Africa / Wendy Vierow.
    v. cm. — (The atlas of the seven continents)
Includes bibliographical references and index.
Contents: Earth's continents and oceans — Africa long ago — How to read a map — Natural wonders of Africa — Countries of Africa — The climate of Africa — Africa's plants and animals — Making a living in Africa — The people of Africa — A scientist in Africa.
ISBN 0-8239-6687-9 (lib. bdg.)
1. Africa–Geography–Juvenile literature. 2. Africa–Maps for children. [1. Africa. 2. Maps.] I. Title.
DT6.7 .V54 2004
916—dc21

                                    2002154690

Manufactured in the United States of America

 Contents

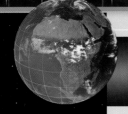

Earth's Continents and Oceans

Africa is one of seven continents on Earth. A continent is a large body of land. The map on the next page shows Earth's seven continents. They are Africa, Antarctica, Asia, Australia, Europe, North America, and South America. The map also shows Earth's oceans. An ocean is a large body of salt water. The Arctic, Atlantic, Indian, and Pacific are Earth's oceans. Some people believe that the waters around Antarctica form a fifth ocean called the Southern Ocean.

More than 200 million years ago, Earth's continents were all part of one giant continent called Pangaea. Pangaea was surrounded by one ocean called Panthalassa. Over time, Pangaea broke into smaller continents. This is because Earth's surface is always changing. Even today, the continents are still moving. Africa has been moving toward Europe for millions of years. Scientists think that the movement of the continents is caused by Earth's **plates**. These plates float on partly melted rock, deep inside Earth. When Earth's plates move, they cause changes on Earth's surface. Mountains and volcanoes are created, and **earthquakes** can occur.

North America

Atlantic Ocean

Arctic Ocean

Europe

Asia

Africa

South America

Indian Ocean

Australia

Pacific Ocean

Antarctica

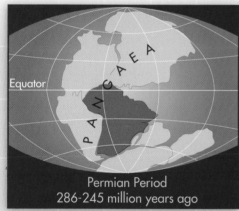

Permian Period
286-245 million years ago

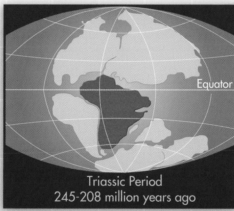

Triassic Period
245-208 million years ago

Jurassic Period
208-144 million years ago

As Pangaea began to break up, it formed continents known as Laurasia and Gondwanaland. Millions of years later, Earth's movement caused these continents to form the seven continents on Earth today. The part that became Africa is shown in red.

Cretaceous Period
144-66 million years ago

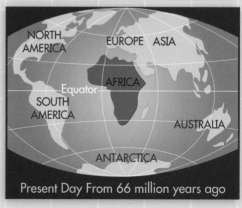

Present Day From 66 million years ago

Africa Long Ago

Dinosaurs lived in what is now Africa during the Mesozoic **era**, a period of time about 245 million to 66 million years ago. The Mesozoic era is also known as the Age of Dinosaurs. It was a time when dinosaurs and other reptiles were the largest animals on Earth. Scientists learn about dinosaurs and African life of long ago by studying **fossils**.

During the Mesozoic era, fish, including a shark called *Hybodus*, swam in African waters. Pterosaurs, or flying reptiles, flew in African skies. *Rhamphorhynchus*, a fishing pterosaur with a pointed beak, caught slippery water animals. Another pterosaur called *Pterodactylus* ate worms. On the island of Madagascar lived *Majungatholus*, a meat-eating dinosaur that was as large as an elephant. On what is now the mainland of Africa, plant-eating and meat-eating dinosaurs searched for food. Brachiosaurs, huge dinosaurs, probably ate conifers, or trees with cones. Other plants of the Mesozoic era were cycads, or trees that looked like palms or ferns, and ginkgo trees. The first flowering plants appeared at the end of the Mesozoic era.

This is a painting of a Majungatholus, a dinosuar that lived from 70 million to 65 million years ago. Fossils of the powerful Majungatholus have been found on the African island of Madagascar. This 30-foot (9-m) meat-eater preferred to dine on sauropods, which were long-necked, plant-eating dinosaurs.

How to Read a Map

There are many kinds of maps. For example, there are road maps that show the streets and the highways of a city or a state. You can find maps of a whole continent, such as Africa, that show its mountains, lakes, rivers, and other kinds of land and water. Some maps show how much rain a place may receive. Other maps show the kinds of products that are grown or made in a certain location.

You can find different maps in an atlas. Maps have many features that can help you to read them. The title tells what the map shows. Often the title is located in the map key, or legend. A map key or legend also tells what certain **symbols** on the map mean.

You can tell how the size of a map compares to the actual size of a place by looking at the map's **scale**. The map's **compass rose**, or **north pointer**, shows direction. The four main directions on Earth are north, south, east, and west. North is the direction toward the North Pole. Longitude lines, which show the position of a location on a map, run north and south. Latitude lines also show position on a map, but these lines run east and west. The **equator** is 0° latitude.

Natural Wonders of Africa

Africa has many different landforms. The most famous is the Sahara, the world's largest desert. It covers about 3,500,000 square miles (9,064,958 sq km). That's almost as big as the United States! The Sahara is in northern Africa. The Kalahari and Namib Deserts are in the southern part of Africa. Between these deserts lie grasslands called savannas. In the middle of the continent are **rain forests**. One of the thickest rain forests in the world is in the northern part of the Democratic Republic of the Congo. There are several African mountain ranges, including the Atlas Mountains in northern Africa and the Drakensberg Mountains in southern Africa. Africa's highest mountain, Mount Kilimanjaro, is in eastern Africa and towers at 19,341 feet (5,895 m). The Great Rift Valley lies between two lines of eastern mountains. This huge valley, which stretches north to south about 4,000 miles (6,437 km), is a source of early human fossils. Africa has many famous bodies of water. The Nile River, the world's longest river, flows 4,160 miles (6,695 km). Africa's longest freshwater lake, Lake Tanganyika, is 410 miles (660 km) long.

1 Lake Tanganyika, Lake Victoria, Great Rift Valley

2 Mount Kilimanjaro's snowcap and glaciers

3 Egypt and the Nile Delta

4 The Congo Basin

AFRICA: LAND AND WATER

Atlantic Ocean

Mediterranean Sea

ATLAS MOUNTAINS

LIBYAN DESERT

Ahaggat Mountains

SAHARA

Nile River

Red Sea

Niger River

Niger River

Lake Chad

White Nile River

Blue Nile River

RIFT VALLEY

CONGO

Virunga Mountains

Congo

BASIN

RIFT VALLEY

Lake Victoria

Lake Tanganyika

Kilimanjaro

EQUATOR

RIFT VALLEY

N

Atlantic Ocean

NAMIB DESERT

Zambezi River

Zambezi River

KALAHARI DESERT

Drakensberg Mountains

Indian Ocean

0 km 300 600 900 km
scale at the Equator
Mercator Projection

GEOATLAS · Copyright 1998 Graphi-Ogre

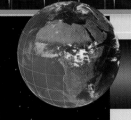

Countries of Africa

Africa has 53 countries. They range in size from the largest country of Sudan, which is 967,500 square miles (2,505,813.5 sq km), to the smallest country of Seychelles, which consists of about 115 islands and is 176 square miles (456 sq km). At one time, many different European countries had colonies in Africa. Africa was rich in many **resources** that Europeans wanted, such as **minerals** and palm oil. Today some islands that lie off the coast of Africa still belong to the European countries of France, Portugal, Spain, and the United Kingdom. By the 1960s, most of European rule ended in Africa. Some African countries have more than one capital city. For example, South Africa has three capital cities. Cape Town is the legislative capital where government leaders meet. The legislative part of a government has the power to make or pass laws. Pretoria is the administrative capital, where government departments have their headquarters and manage their businesses. Bloemfontein is the judicial capital, where South Africa's highest court of law meets.

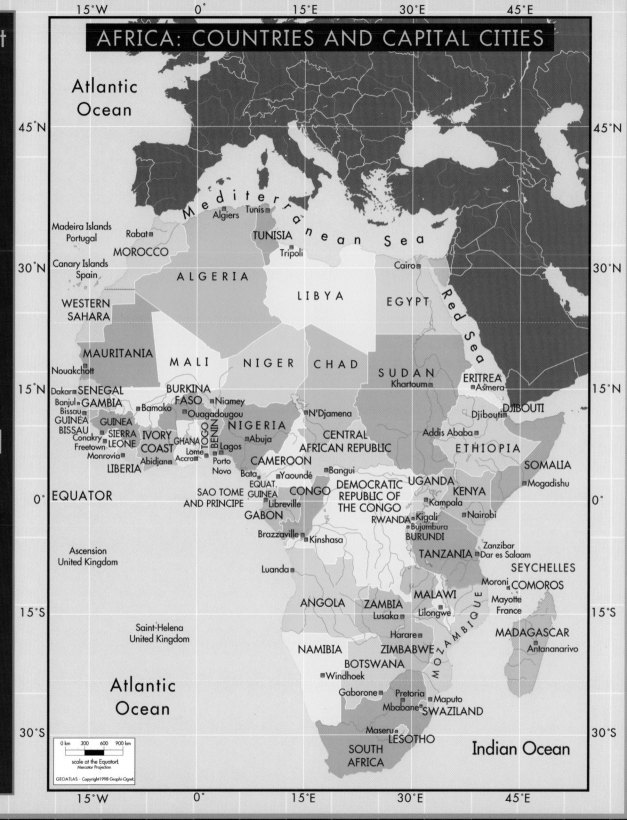

Africa's Largest Capital Cities

■ Capital Cities

Cairo, Egypt
6,800,000

Kinshasa, Dem. Rep. of
4,655,000 the Congo

Abidjan, Cote d'Ivoire
2,500,000

Cape Town, South Africa
2,415,000

Addis Ababa, Ethiopia
2,113,000

Europe-owned Islands

Azores
(Portugal)
Madeira Islands
(Portugal)
Canary Islands
(Spain)
Ascension
(United Kingdom)
St. Helena
(United Kingdom)
Réunion
(France)

AFRICA: COUNTRIES AND CAPITAL CITIES

Atlantic Ocean

Mediterranean Sea

Algiers
Tunis
TUNISIA
Tripoli
Rabat
Madeira Islands
Portugal
MOROCCO
Canary Islands
Spain
ALGERIA
LIBYA
EGYPT
Cairo
Red Sea
WESTERN
SAHARA
MAURITANIA
MALI
NIGER
CHAD
SUDAN
ERITREA
Nouakchott
Khartoum
Asmera
Dakar
SENEGAL
BURKINA
FASO
Niamey
N'Djamena
DJIBOUTI
Banjul
GAMBIA
Bamako
Ouagadougou
NIGERIA
Djibouti
Bissau
GUINEA
BISSAU
GUINEA
SIERRA
LEONE
IVORY
COAST
GHANA
TOGO
BENIN
Abuja
CENTRAL
AFRICAN REPUBLIC
Addis Ababa
ETHIOPIA
Conakry
Freetown
Lome
Lagos
Accra
Porto
Novo
CAMEROON
Bangui
SOMALIA
Monrovia
Abidjan
Yaoundé
Mogadishu
LIBERIA
Bata
EQUAT.
GUINEA
SAO TOME
AND PRINCIPE
CONGO
DEMOCRATIC
REPUBLIC OF
THE CONGO
UGANDA
KENYA
EQUATOR
Libreville
Kampala
GABON
Nairobi
RWANDA
Kigali
Brazzaville
Bujumbura
BURUNDI
Kinshasa
TANZANIA
Zanzibar
Dar es Salaam
Ascension
United Kingdom
Luanda
SEYCHELLES
Moroni
COMOROS
ANGOLA
ZAMBIA
MALAWI
Mayotte
France
Saint-Helena
United Kingdom
Lusaka
Lilongwe
Harare
MADAGASCAR
Antananarivo
NAMIBIA
ZIMBABWE
MOZAMBIQUE
BOTSWANA
Atlantic
Ocean
Windhoek
Gaborone
Pretoria
Maputo
Mbabane
SWAZILAND
Maseru
LESOTHO
Indian Ocean
SOUTH
AFRICA

0 km   300   600   900 km
scale at the Equator.
Mercator Projection
GEOATLAS - Copyright1998 Graphi-Ogret.

15°W   0°   15°E   30°E   45°E
45°N
30°N
15°N
0°
15°S
30°S

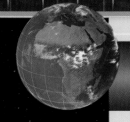

The Climate of Africa

Most of Africa has a warm climate with rain that varies greatly from place to place. Climate means all the weather that occurs in one place over a long time. Climate includes temperature, or how hot or cold a place is, and precipitation, or how much moisture falls from the sky. The precipitation in the Sahara amounts to an average of less than 4 inches (10 cm) of rain each year. Compare this to the precipitation in the hills around Mount Cameroon, where an average of 394 inches (1,001 cm) of rain falls yearly.

Places near large bodies of water are cooler in the summer and warmer in the winter. Elevation, or how high a place is, also affects climate. Most places at high elevations have a cool, wet climate. Places closest to the equator are warm and wet. Because the equator runs through the middle of Africa, Africa has more **tropical** areas than any other continent. Tropical climates are always warm. The hottest recorded temperature on Earth was in Africa. In 1922, it was 136°F (58°C) in the shade in Al Aziziyah, Libya!

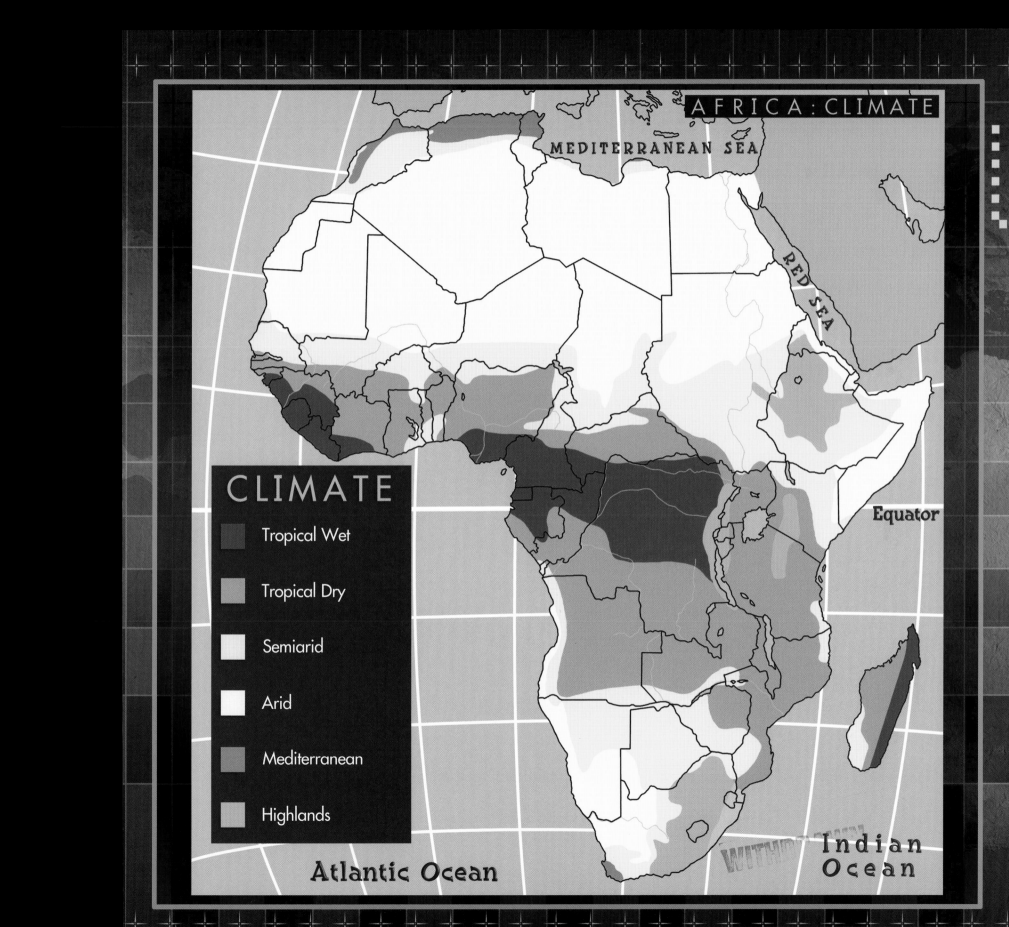

MEDITERRANEAN SEA

RED SEA

Equator

CLIMATE

Tropical Wet

Tropical Dry

Semiarid

Arid

Mediterranean

Highlands

Atlantic Ocean

Indian Ocean

Africa's Plants and Animals

Africa has many wild animals and plants. In the deserts, there are **oases** where date palms, doum palms, tamarisks, and acacia trees grow. Many animals live in the African grasslands. These include elephants, lions, and cheetahs. Also in the grasslands are acacia and broad-trunked baobab trees. Monkeys, chimpanzees, gorillas, and leopards live in the African rain forests near the equator. Oil palms, fruit trees, ebony trees, and mahogany trees grow there. The island of Madagascar has chameleons, long-tailed lemurs, and tenrecs. Some tenrecs look like mice. Others look like porcupines.

Traders and colonists brought plants and animals from other parts of the world to Africa. Plants such as bananas, corn, cacaos, and teas, and animals such as cattle, goats, sheep, and camels are not native to Africa. Many of these animals and plants are raised on farms. Sometimes, Africa's wild animals destroy crops or attack farm animals. However, many African countries are trying to protect wildlife by creating parks and limiting hunting.

These animals and plants are found in many places on the continent of Africa.

AFRICA'S ANIMALS

Lion cub in the grasslands

Lowland gorilla in the Congo

Cape zebra in South Africa

Addax

Cheetah in the grasslands.

African elephant

Rain forest chimpanzee

Cacao tree

Banana tree

Giraffe

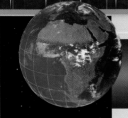

Making a Living in Africa

Most people in Africa grow crops or raise animals for their own use. In tropical areas farmers grow bananas, rice, and yams. However, some farmers raise goods to sell to people in other countries. In western Africa farmers grow cacao beans, which are used to make chocolate, cocoa, and cocoa butter. Africa is the world's leader in growing and selling cacao beans. Farmers also sell bananas, which they grow in the forests of central Africa, to other countries. Uganda is a leading producer of bananas worldwide. Africa's rivers, lakes, and oceans provide plenty of fish for the continent's fishing **industry**.

Some of the continent's greatest resources come from mines. Mines in South Africa produce the most gold in the world. Diamonds and other products, such as copper, **uranium**, and natural gas, are also found in South Africa, Nigeria, and Zambia. Many countries around the world get their oil from Algeria, Libya, and Nigeria.

There is very little manufacturing in Africa. South Africa makes most of Africa's goods, including automobiles, clothing, and chemicals.

A worker checks pipes in a Libyan oil field. Selling oil to other countries provides 50 percent of Libya's earnings.

Fishermen pull in a fishing net from the sea on the coast of Sierra Leone.

Workers harvest cacao beans in the Democratic Republic of the Congo.

The People of Africa

Scientists believe that the first people on Earth lived in Africa about two million years ago. Today more than 800 **ethnic groups** live in Africa. Most groups have their own way of life and their own language. In the north most Africans are **Arabs**. A small group of Arabs are **bedouins**. They live in small groups in the Sahara, herding sheep, goats, and camels.

In some parts of Africa, ethnic groups have the same name as the language that they speak. For example, in some West African countries, a people called Yoruba speak Yoruba. Today some people in North America and South America have **ancestors** who spoke West African languages. This is because these languages were spoken by thousands of West Africans who were taken to the Americas as slaves hundreds of years ago. Today most Africans live in the country rather than in cities. Some own or rent farms. Others live in villages surrounded by farmland. Of the Africans who live in cities, the largest number live in Cairo, Egypt. More than 5,000 years ago, Egypt was one of the world's greatest **civilizations**.

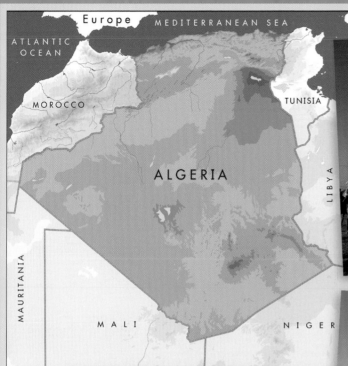

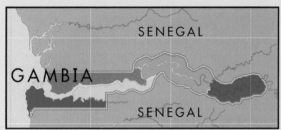

These Berber men of North Africa ride their camels near the Hoggar Mountains in Algeria.

These school children in the West African country of Gambia pose for the camera.

This young woman from Kenya, in East Africa, is dressed in the clothing of the Masai people.

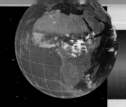

A Scientist in Africa

About 90 percent of the people who suffer from malaria, a dangerous **disease**, are from Africa. Most are children. Malaria kills more than one million people around the world every year. People with malaria develop a high fever and chills. Dr. Theonest Mutabingwa, of Muheza, Tanzania, studies malaria, which people can get if they are bitten by mosquitoes carrying certain parasites. Parasites are harmful creatures that feed on other living things. Doctors use special drugs to treat malaria. However, malaria parasites have built a resistance to these drugs. This means drugs that once worked well are no longer effective. Dr. Mutabingwa led a team of **researchers** in Tanzania who tested a new drug called Lapdap on young children with malaria. They found that 93 percent of the children using the new drug were cured of malaria. Scientists worry that malaria parasites will build a resistance to the new drug. They hope to find a **vaccine**, or shot that prevents people from ever getting the disease. In the meantime, Dr. Mutabingwa's studies might help to treat people with malaria throughout the world.

Glossary

ancestors (AN-ses-terz) Relatives who lived long ago.

Arabs (AR-ubz) Members of a group of people who live in southern Asia or northern Africa.

bedouins (BEH-duh-wunz) Members of certain groups who live in the deserts of northern Africa.

civilizations (sih-vih-lih-ZAY-shunz) People living in an organized way.

compass rose (KUM-pus ROHZ) A drawing on a map that shows directions.

disease (duh-ZEEZ) Illness or sickness.

earthquakes (URTH-kwayks) Shakings of Earth's crust caused by plates running into each other.

equator (ih-KWAY-tur) An imaginary line around Earth that separates it into two parts.

era (ER-uh) A period of time or history.

ethnic groups (ETH-nik GROOPS) Groups of people who have the same race, culture, or language, or who belong to the same country.

fossils (FAH-sulz) The hardened remains of dead animals or plants.

industry (IN-dus-tree) A moneymaking business in which many people work and make money producing a particular product.

minerals (MIH-ner-ulz) Natural elements that are not animals, plants, or other living things.

north pointer (NORTH POYNT-er) A drawing on a map that shows the direction of the North Pole.

oases (oh-AY-seez) Areas in a desert where plants can grow because of a water source.

plates (PLAYTS) The moving pieces of Earth's crust.

rain forests (RAYN FOR-ests) Thick forests that receive large amounts of rain during the year.

researchers (REE-serch-erz) People who carefully study something to find out more about it.

resources (REE-sors-ez) Supplies or sources of energy or useful materials.

scale (SKAYL) The measurements on a map compared to actual measurements on Earth.

symbols (SIM-bulz) Objects or designs that stand for something else.

tropical (TRAH-puh-kul) Having to do with the warm parts of Earth that are near the equator.

uranium (yoo-RAY-nee-um) A heavy metallic element that gives off rays of energy.

vaccine (vak-SEEN) A shot that keeps a person from getting a certain sickness.

Index

Web Sites

Due to the changing nature of Internet links, PowerKids Press has developed an online list of Web sites related to the subject of this book. This site is updated regularly. Please use this link to access the list:
www.powerkidslinks.com/asc/africa/